MINI
A DOZEN A DAY
SONGBOOK

Easy Classical

Including music from Bach, Chopin, Elgar, Handel,
Mozart, Tchaikovsky, plus many more...

ISBN 978-1-78038-910-3

WILLIS MUSIC

EXCLUSIVELY DISTRIBUTED BY

HAL•LEONARD®

Visit Hal Leonard Online at
www.halleonard.com

World headquarters, contact:
Hal Leonard
7777 West Bluemound Road
Milwaukee, WI 53213
Email: info@halleonard.com

In Europe, contact:
Hal Leonard Europe Limited
1 Red Place
London, W1K 6PL
Email: info@halleonardeurope.com

In Australia, contact:
Hal Leonard Australia Pty. Ltd.
4 Lentara Court
Cheltenham, Victoria, 3192 Australia
Email: info@halleonard.com.au

This collection of well-known classical pieces can be used on its own or as supplementary material to the iconic *A Dozen A Day* techniques series by Edna Mae Burnam. The pieces have been arranged to progress gradually, applying concepts and patterns from Burnam's technical exercises whenever possible. Teacher accompaniments and suggested guidelines for use with the original series are also provided.

These arrangements are excellent supplements for any method and may also be used for sight-reading practice for more advanced students.

The difficulty titles of certain editions of the *A Dozen A Day* books may vary internationally. This repertoire book corresponds to the first difficulty level.

Contents

Track no.

Air On The G String Johann Sebastian Bach 30   **19–20**

Ave Verum Corpus, K618 Wolfgang Amadeus Mozart 28   **17–18**

Canon in D Johann Pachelbel 6   **3–4**

Gymnopédie No. 1 Erik Satie 15   **9–10**

Largo (from *Xerxes*) George Frideric Handel 24   **15–16**

Largo (from *From The New World*) Antonín Dvořák 21   **13–14**

Morning Mood (from *Peer Gynt*) Edvard Grieg 18   **11–12**

Ode To Joy (from *Symphony No. 9, Fourth Movement*)
Ludwig Van Beethoven 8   **5–6**

Panis Angelicus César Franck 3   **1–2**

Theme from Swan Lake Pyotr Ilyich Tchaikovsky 12   **7–8**

Panis Angelicus

Use with A Dozen A Day Mini Book, after Group I (page 8)

Composed by César Franck
Arranged by Christopher Hussey

TRACKS 1–2

Cantabile

Cantabile

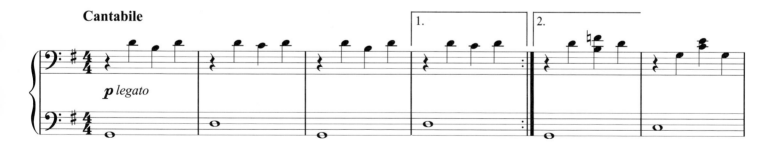

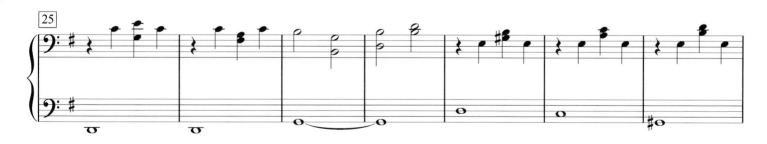

Canon in D

Use after Group I (page 8)

Composed by Johann Pachelbel
Arranged by Christopher Hussey

TRACKS 3–4

Andante

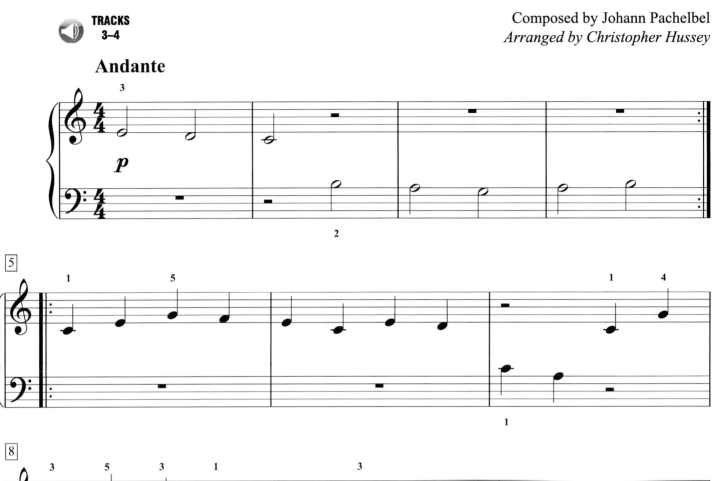

Andante

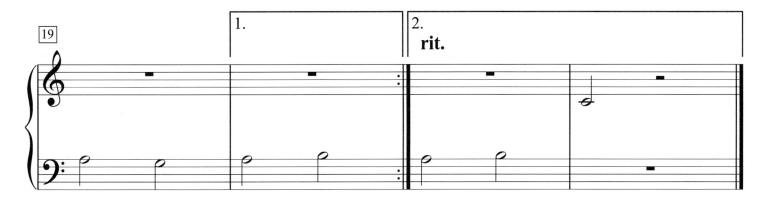

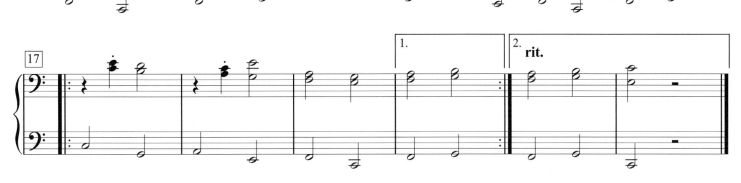

Ode To Joy

from SYMPHONY No.9, FOURTH MOVEMENT

Use after Group II (page 12)

Composed by Ludwig Van Beethoven
Arranged by Christopher Hussey

TRACKS
5–6

Allegro

4

Allegro

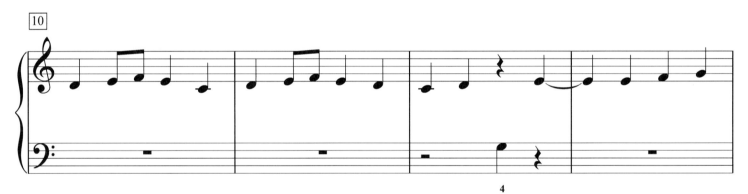

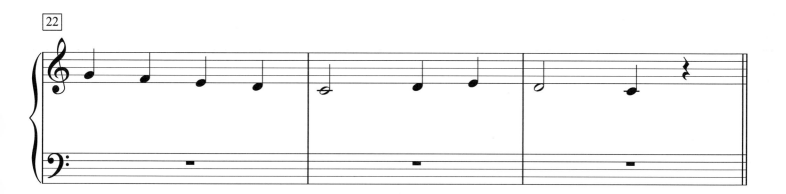

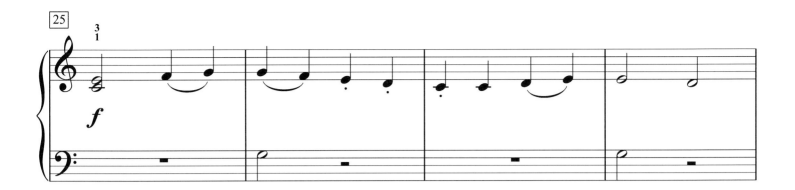

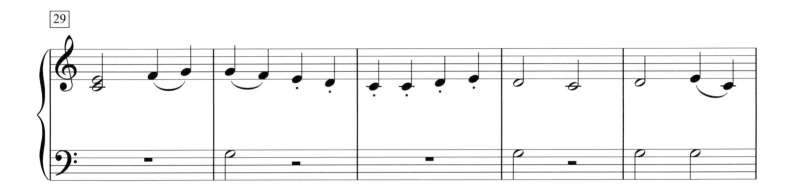

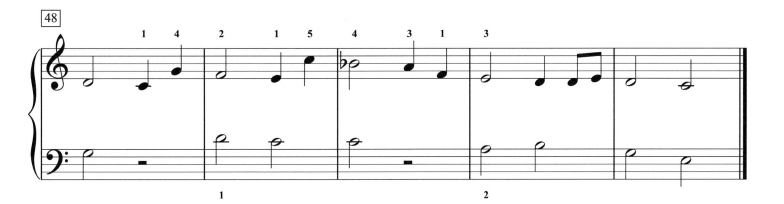

Theme from Swan Lake

Use after Group III (page 16)

Composed by Pyotr Ilyich Tchaikovsky
Arranged by Christopher Hussey

TRACKS 7–8

Moderato

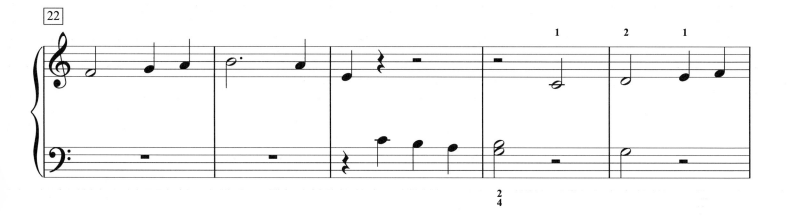

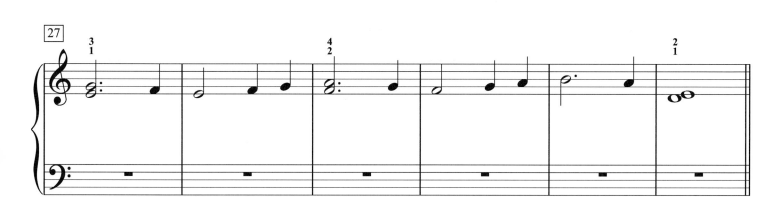

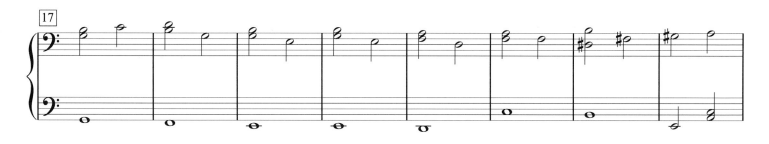

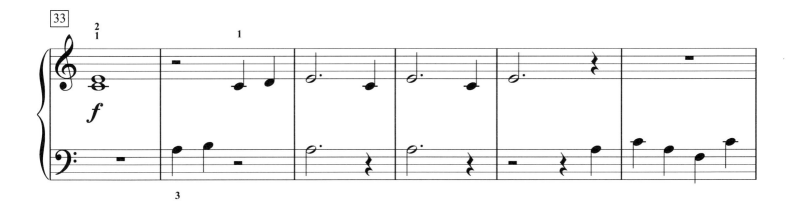

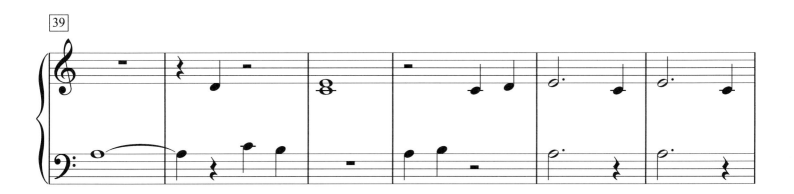

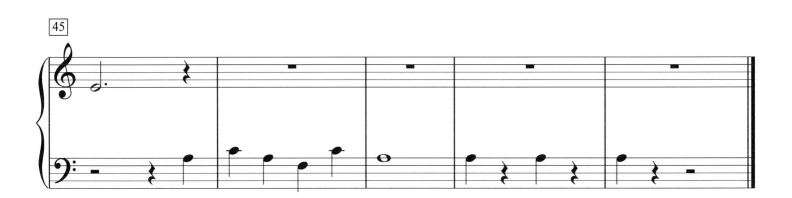

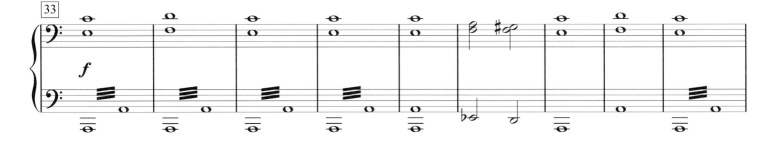

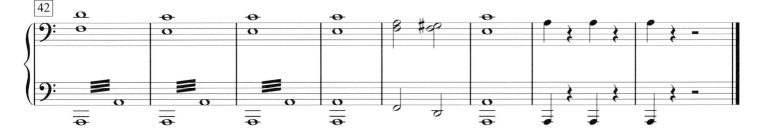

Gymnopédie No.1

Use after Group IV (page 20)

Composed by Erik Satie
Arranged by Christopher Hussey

TRACKS 9–10

Lento

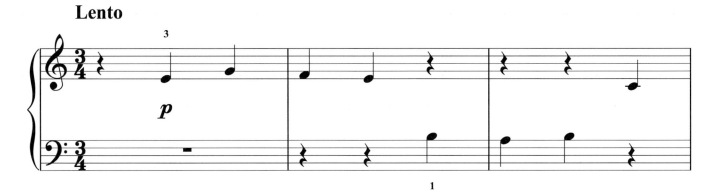

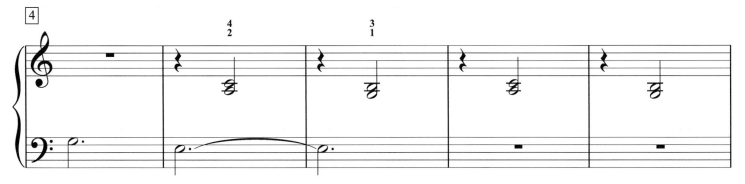

Lento

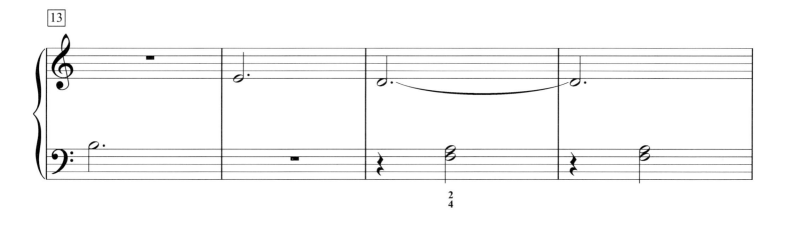

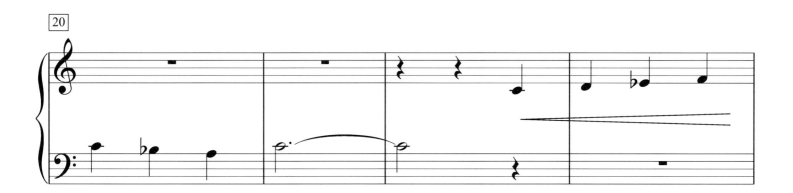

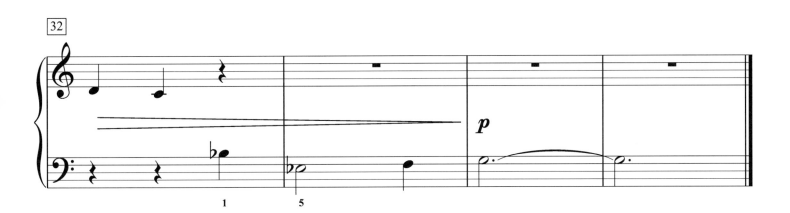

Morning Mood
from PEER GYNT

Use after Group IV (page 20)

Composed by Edvard Grieg
Arranged by Christopher Hussey

TRACKS
11–12

Grazioso

Grazioso

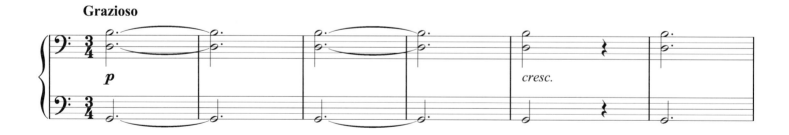

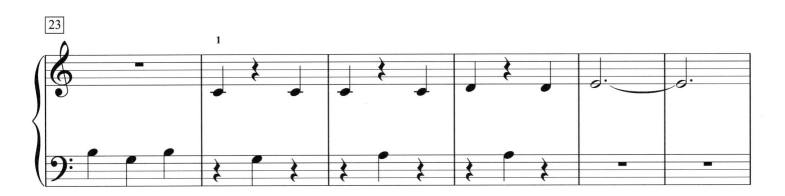

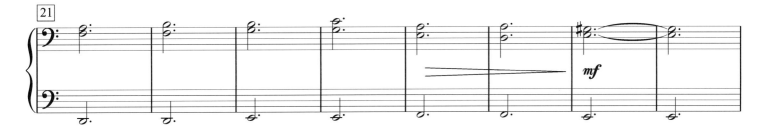

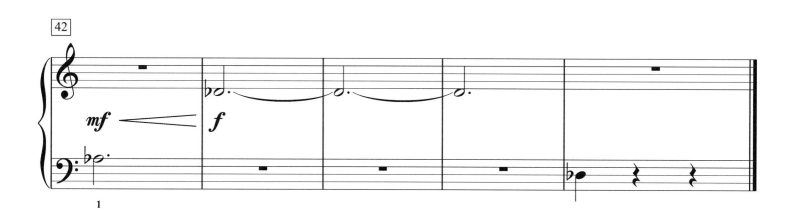

Largo
from FROM THE NEW WORLD

Use after Group IV (page 20)

Composed by Antonín Dvořák
Arranged by Christopher Hussey

TRACKS
13–14

Teneramente

Teneramente

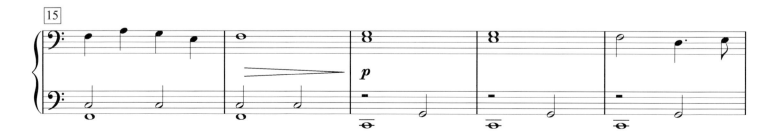

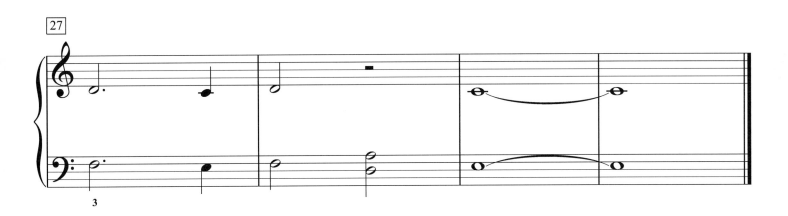

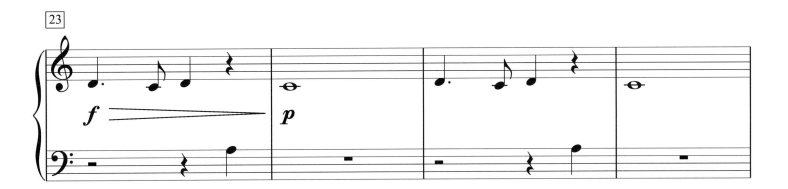

Largo
from XERXES

Use after Group V (page 24)

TRACKS
15–16

Composed by George Frideric Handel
Arranged by Christopher Hussey

Largo

Largo

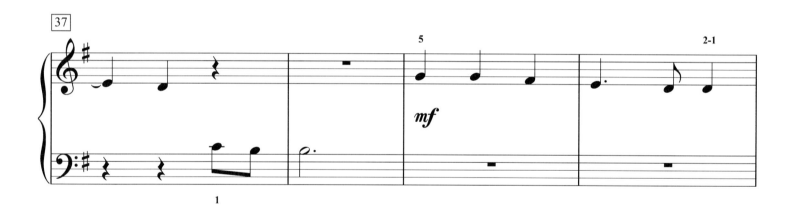

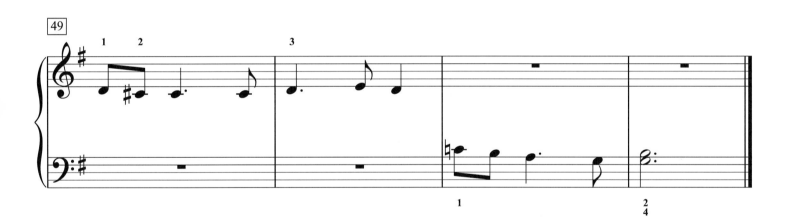

Ave Verum Corpus, K618

Use after Group V (page 24)

TRACKS
17–18

Composed by Wolfgang Amadeus Mozart
Arranged by Christopher Hussey

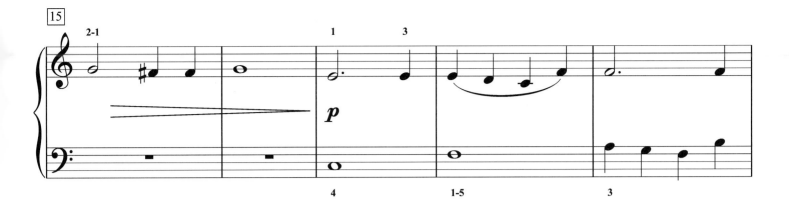

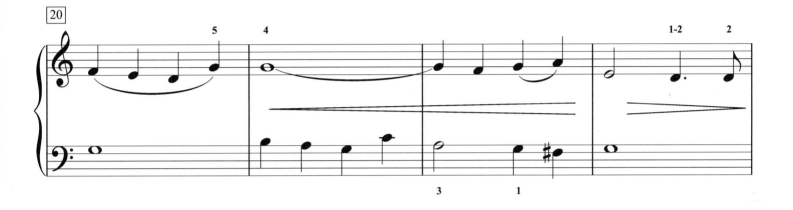

Air On The G String

Use after Group V (page 24)

TRACKS
19–20

Composed by Johann Sebastian Bach
Arranged by Christopher Hussey

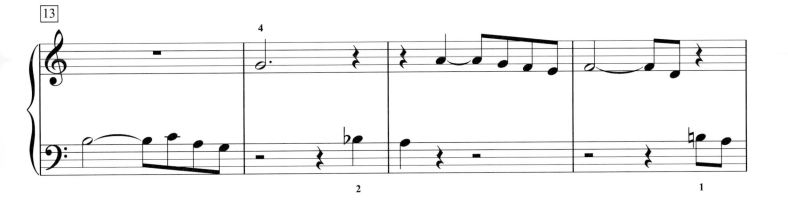